~ *A* SEASON OF SUNDAYS '98 ~

Images of the 1998 Gaelic games year by the *Sportsfile* team
of photographers, with captions by Tom Humphries

Aer Lingus  RTÉ sportsfile

An Official GAA publication, published by Sportsfile, in association with RTÉ and supported by Aer Lingus

Aer Lingus

WINNING PERFORMANCE

EVERY TIME

Aer Lingus is proud to be associated with Sportsfile in the production of this magnificent pictorial record of the 1998 Gaelic Games season. Every aspect of the year is captured by the expert eye, from the commitment of the players to the fanatical loyalty of the spectators; from the unbounded joy of victory to the deep desolation of defeat. The various codes, competitions, venues and characters of these extraordinary games are all here in this comprehensive compendium that will enrich our memories for many years to come.

Each season that passes, it seems, could not possibly attain the same heights of drama, passion and skill as the previous one. Yet we continue to be astounded by the consistently high levels of achievement reached by people who are truly committed to what they do. It is this total determination to succeed coupled with an obvious love of what they are doing that enables these players to produce high quality performances consistently. It is this unique combination that also produces something extra when required and that creates a strong bond of loyalty between player and supporter. This is what makes our games special and raises them beyond the ordinary to create a special and memorable experience.

In Aer Lingus we know about these things. We understand the importance of quality, commitment and a determination to always raise our game when the occasion demands it. This, we believe, is what makes us stand out from the competition and wins loyalty from our supporters.

You might almost say it is intuitive with us. We believe it is what separates the merely good from the truly great. It is this determination to always produce that something extra that pushes us to strive for that winning performance every time.

GARRY CULLEN
GROUP CHIEF EXECUTIVE, AER LINGUS

A PHOTOGRAPHIC RECORD OF

THE YEAR'S ACTIVITIES

Seosamh Mac Donncha

SEOSAMH MACDONNCHA
UACHTARÁN, CUMANN LÚTHCLEAS GAEL

The current popularity of Gaelic Games is reflected in the proliferation of G.A.A. publications of quality appearing on a continuous basis. However, until late last year there was a glaring void in the ever expanding Gaelic Games library. There was no comprehensive photographic record of the year's activities in circulation.

This omission was addressed in the most effective and imaginative of ways by Ray McManus and his expert lensmen in Sportsfile with the publication of 'A Season of Sundays'. It captured the drama, colour, skill and fervour of a complete season, crystallised between covers for the first time.

It has proved immensely popular with followers of Gaelic Games everywhere. In my travels to our clubs and cities in Europe, North America and Australia, I could not help but notice the consistent presence of 'A Season of Sundays', testimony indeed of what a visual still record presented with powerful imagery can mean to our immigrants.

It has been however not just popular abroad. It has also been a greatly prized possession of a great number of our supporters in Ireland. I am therefore delighted that Sportsfile are again providing a photographic record of the 1998 season in this book, 'A Season of Sundays '98'. I am looking forward to it in anticipation and I am indeed honoured to be associated with it.

Míle buíochas díobh go léir agus Rath Dé ar an obair

Photographers

Ray McManus, David Maher, Brendan Moran, Matt Browne, Damien Eagers and Ray Lohan

Captions

Tom Humphries, The Irish Times

Statistics

Brian Carthy, Gaelic Games Correspondent, RTE

Photographers' Portrait

Angela Smyth at GR Watts Dublin

Design

The Design Gang, Tralee

Colour Reproduction

Newsfax

Printed in Ireland

Kilkenny People Printing Limited

Published by

SPORTSFILE

Patterson House

14 South Circular Road

Portobello

Dublin 8

Ireland

ISBN: 0-9523551-2-4

sportsfile

RAY MCMANUS, DAVID MAHER, RAY LOHAN,
MATT BROWNE, DAMIEN EAGERS AND BRENDAN MORAN

SAFEGUARDING THE MEMORIES

As we are daily subjected to a bombardment of disposable visual images, the power of a printed photograph is more potent than ever. It allows for close, personal scrutiny of an incident and recalls the emotion of that moment for all time. As our photographers release the shutter, they freeze in time a momentous score; a crunching tackle; a balletic leap – all that is dramatic and exciting about our national games.

Like the players, we are seeking to excel; hoping to capture the essence of a game in a single frame. And like the participants, we travel the country, hail rain or snow.

On behalf of the Sportsfile team I present this collection from the 1998 Gaelic Games year, as our record of what was another memorable season of Sundays, and indeed the occasional Saturday. I hope that, with the support of Aer Lingus, our photographs together with the astute commentary of Tom Humphries make for a fitting tribute to the endeavours of the players and officials who train for, and play in the games throughout the year.
Enjoy.

RAY MCMANUS
SPORTSFILE

Good players are always thinking about what they're doing. Great players aren't.

There's no substitute for intuition. It's what separates the merely good from the truly great. It's the ability to always do the most intelligent thing without appearing to give it a moment's thought. It's a gift. And you can't buy it. And you can't fake it. But you can depend on it. When you fly with us.

This is not just an airline.

Longford 0-06 Dublin 0-11   O'Byrne Cup

Who's Who ?... Before the throw-in for the O'Byrne Cup game between Longford and Dublin, photographer Martin Maher checks the identity of officials Kevin Levins and Bob Dohenny as gaelic football experiments with two referees.

O'Byrne Cup   **Carlow 1-07 Wicklow 2-11**

New beginnings. Brian Lacey, once of Tipperary now of Kildare, makes his home debut for his new county in Newbridge. Aidan Dorgan of Cork has the ball though.

Derek Treacy of Carlow rises up there to where the air is rare in the O'Byrne Cup game with Wicklow. Left earthbound beneath him is Darren Burke of Wicklow.

AIB All-Ireland Club Football Semi-Final   **Erin's Isle 2-12   Castlehaven 0-17**

Sarsfields 1-15 Dunloy 1-11   AIB All-Ireland Club Hurling Semi-Final

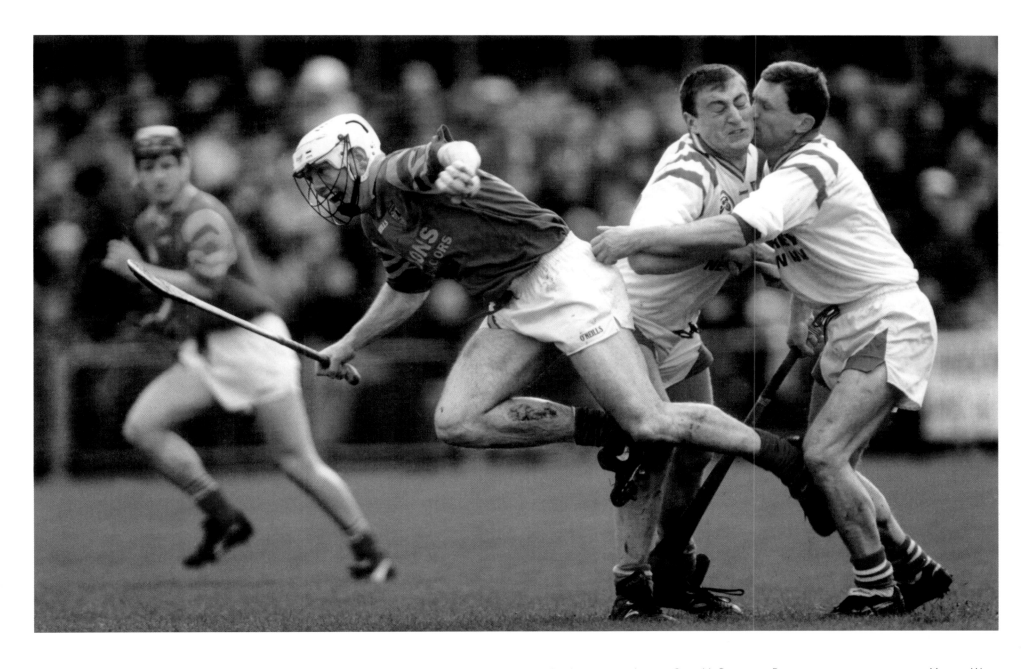

ONE BOUND AND HE'S FREE. COLM MCGUCKIAN OF DUNLOY MAKES GOOD HIS ESCAPE AS MICHAEL WARD
AND GERRY MCGRATH OF SARSFIELDS ARE LEFT DANCING CHEEK TO CHEEK.

EYES FRONT. ERIN'S ISLE DEFENDER KEN SPRATT GETS
A GLOVED FINGER IN FRONT OF CASTLEHAVEN'S COLIN
CROWLEY IN THE ALL-IRELAND CLUB SEMI-FINAL.

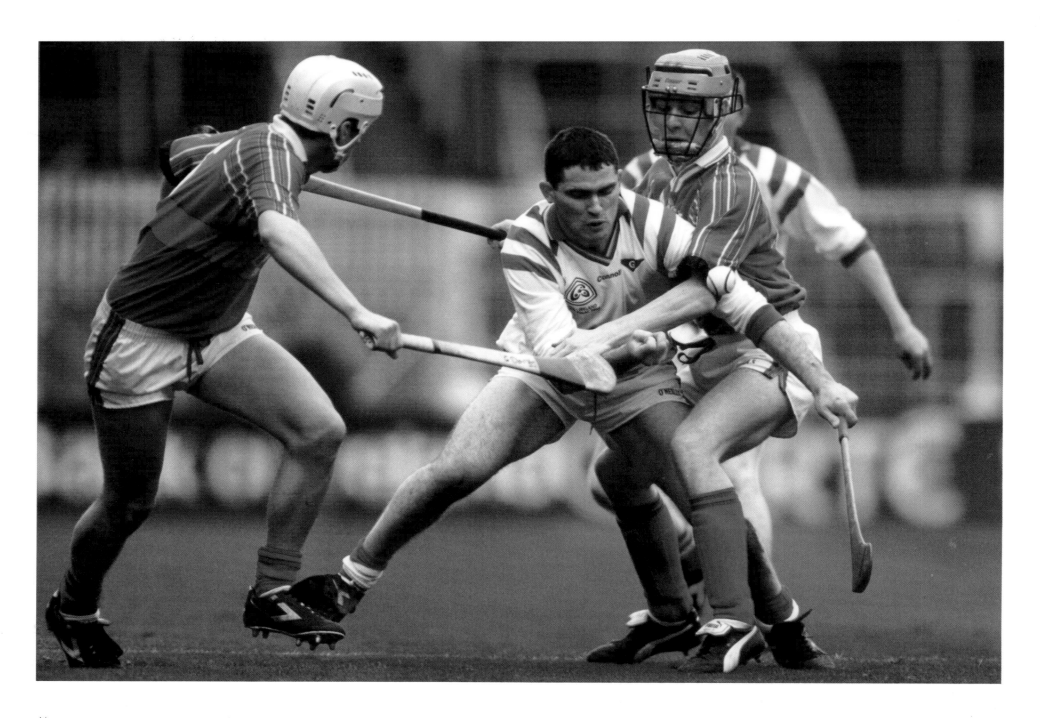

NOTHING MORE THAN A HANDFUL OF DUST. PETER KELLY OF SARSFIELDS IS LEFT WITH NOTHING TO SHOW AS GARETH DOORLEY AND NIALL CLAFFEY OF BIRR CONVERGE ON HIM IN THE ALL-IRELAND FINAL.

Birr 1-13 Sarsfields 0-09   AIB All-Ireland Club Hurling Final

MINE EYES HAVE SEEN THE GLORY. PJ WHELAHAN,
COACH OF THE SUCCESSFUL BIRR TEAM, CELEBRATES
THE ALL-IRELAND SUCCESS OF CLUB AND FAMILY.
PJ'S THREE SONS PLAYED ON THE TEAM ALSO.

March 17

AIB All-Ireland Club Hurling Final   **Birr 1-13 Sarsfields 0-09**

ANOTHER FAMILY AFFAIR. JOE ERRITY, THE BIRR CAPTAIN, WHOSE FATHER TOMMY PASSED AWAY WHILE WATCHING AN EARLIER GAME IN THE CHAMPIONSHIP, RAISES THE TOMMY MOORE CUP IN TRIUMPH.

Corofin 0-15 Erin's Isle 0-10 AIB All-Ireland Club Football Final

WALLFLOWER AT THE BIG DANCE. CHARLIE REDMOND WATCHES THE PLAYERS AND FRIENDS HE GREW UP WITH IN ERIN'S ISLE LINE OUT FOR THE ALL-IRELAND FINAL AS HE SERVES A DISCIPLINARY SUSPENSION.

TREVOR BURKE OF COROFIN AND DAMIEN COLLINS OF ERIN'S ISLE COLLIDE LIKE DODGEMS WHILE KEITH BARR AND AIDAN DONNELLAN MOP UP THE AIR MILES.

Corofin 0-15 Erin's Isle 0-10   AIB All-Ireland Club Football Final

YOU AIN'T SEEN NOTHIN' YET. YOU AIN'T HEARD NOTHIN' YET. EXUBERANT COROFIN CAPTAIN RAY SILKE CLEARS HIS THROAT BEFORE HIS FIRST BIG VICTORY SPEECH OF THE YEAR.

Church and General National Football League Semi-Final   **Offaly 3-10 Donegal 1-14**

YOU KNOW, THEY HAVEN'T GOT THE HUNGER OF THE EIGHTIES TEAM. SIX-YEAR-OLD DANIEL CAREY FROM TULLAMORE SURVEYS HIS COUNTY FOOTBALL SIDE FROM HILL 16.

GO ON YA HANDY THING BERTIE. TWO DAYS AFTER THE BREAKTHROUGH OF THE GOOD FRIDAY AGREEMENT, AN TAOISEACH, BERTIE AHERN, T.D.,
TAKES THE PLAUDITS OF WELL-WISHERS AS HE DRIVES FROM CROKE PARK.

Church and General National Hurling League   **Kilkenny 1-05 Laois 0-13**

He is resurrected. DJ Carey hands referee Pat Aherne the slip of paper as he comes on as a substitute for Adrian Ronan. The appearance is Carey's first since the end of his short-lived retirement.

AFTER THE TRIP TO THE OAK LEAF SUPERSTORE. A DERRY CHILD AND HIS MINDER WATCH THE NATIONAL LEAGUE FINAL UNFOLD.

Church and General National Football League Final **Offaly 0-09 Derry 0-07**

ALL FOR THE LOVE OF THE GAME. THE WEATHER TURNS MEAN AS FERGAL McCUSKER AND DERMOT DOUGAN OF DERRY SANDWICH RONAN MOONEY OF OFFALY. RONAN QUINN AND JOHNNY McBRIDE ARRIVE SHADOWING EACH OTHER.

Offaly 0-09 Derry 0-07   Church and General National Football League Final

FOR THE FAMILY ALBUM. FINBAR CULLEN OF OFFALY LIFTS THE NATIONAL LEAGUE TROPHY AS GAA PRESIDENT JOE MCDONAGH LOOKS ON.

Church and General National Hurling League Semi-Final **Cork 2-15 Clare 0-10**

STRAINING EYES THAT COULD PICK OUT THE MOTES OF DUST IN THE EARLY SUMMER SUNLIGHT. JOE DEANE OF CORK DRAWS ON THE BALL AS BRIAN LOHAN OF CLARE CONVERGES WITH INTENT.

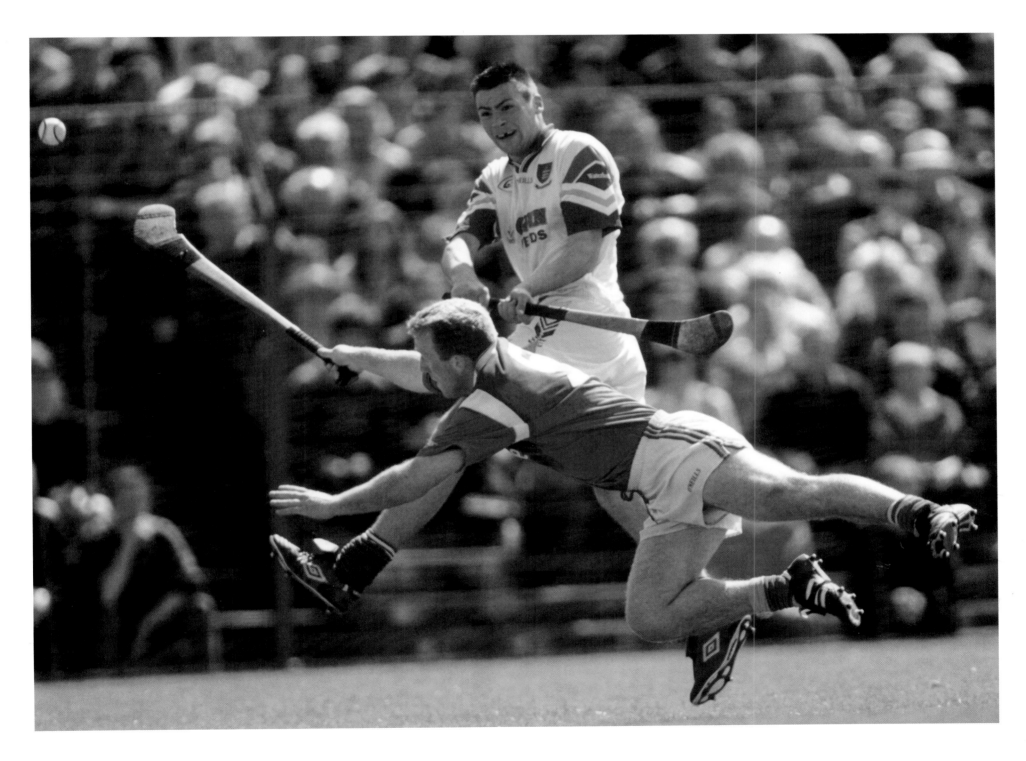

KEN McGRATH OF WATERFORD WALKS ON AIR AS LIMERICK'S DAVE CLARKE MAKES A DESPAIRING ATTEMPT AT A FLYING BLOCK.

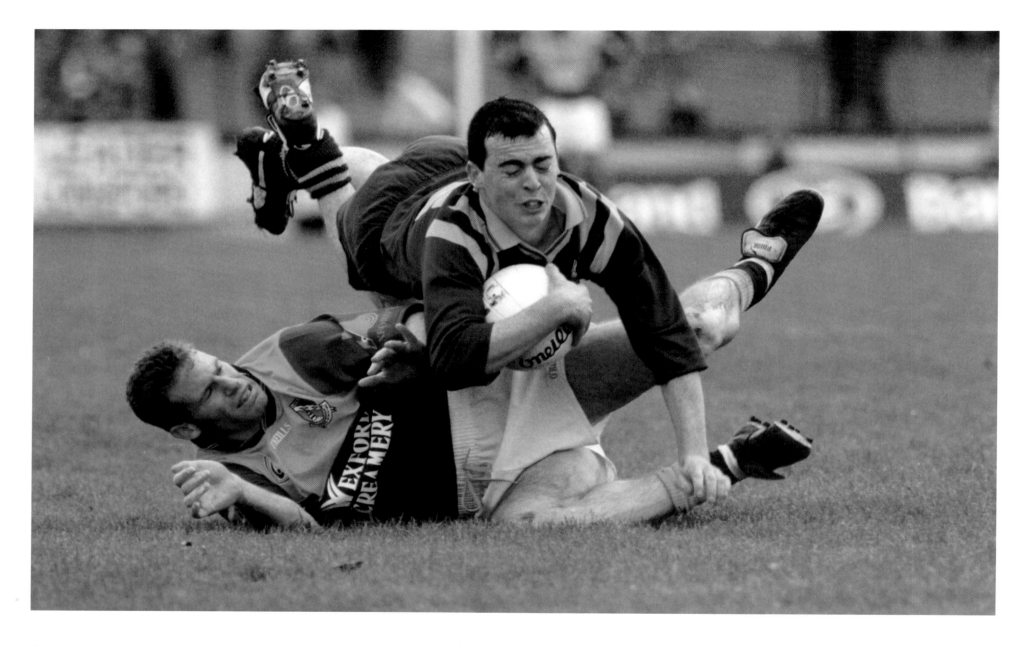

PADRAIC DAVIS OF LONGFORD FLIES RUGBY STYLE OVER WEXFORD DEFENDER CIARAN ROCHE.

Down 0-15 Tyrone 2-07   Bank of Ireland Ulster Football Championship

HAVE YE ANY OLD TICKLES STEPHEN, ANY OLD TICKLES AT ALL.
MICHEÁL MAGILL AND SIMON POLLAND OF DOWN TRY TO
PERSUADE STEPHEN LAWN TO PART WITH THE BALL.

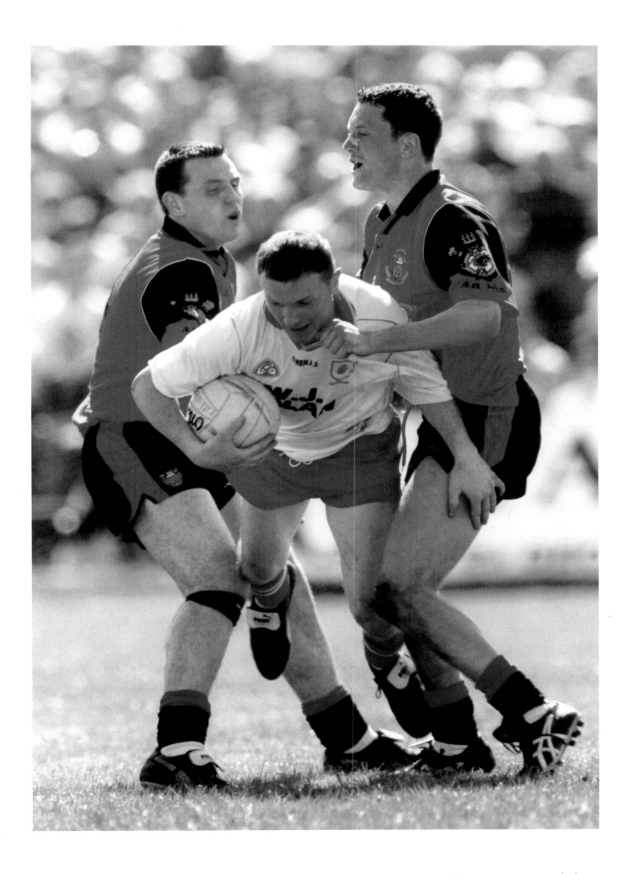

May 17

Church and General National Hurling League Final   **Cork 2-14 Waterford 0-13**

GET YOUR OFFICIAL MILLINERY, GET YOUR OFFICIAL MILLINERY.
A HURLING FAN SUFFERS THE SUN IN THURLES.

Cork 2-14 Waterford 0-13   Church and General National Hurling League Final

WATERFORD'S RETURN TO THE BIG TIME DRAWS THEM A MEDIA COMPLIMENT. THE PHOTOGRAPHERS HAVE SENT THEIR FIRST FIFTEEN TO THE GAME.

Church and General National Hurling League Final   **Cork 2-14 Waterford 0-13**

WAITING FOR THE COMFORT OF ANOTHER DAY. WATERFORD COACH SHANE AHERNE COMFORTS DEFENDER BRIAN GREENE AS THEY ABSORB THEIR DEFEAT ON THE PITCH IN THURLES.

*LONG TIME COMING. GOOD TIME COMING. CORK CAPTAIN DIARMUID O'SULLIVAN
AND A SWARM OF COUNTYFOLK CELEBRATE THE ARRIVAL OF A TROPHY AT LAST.*

PARALLELS OVER SPHERE. RAYMOND MAGEE OF MEATH AND BARRY MALONE OF OFFALY LEVITATE OVER THE BALL DURING THEIR SIDES' CHAMPIONSHIP CLASH.

ONE OF THOSE DAYS WHICH ARE LONG ON AGONY AND SHORT ON ECSTASY. OFFALY CORNER-BACK CATHAL DALY LIES INJURED ON THE CROKE PARK TURF.

Meath 3-10 Offaly 0-07   Bank of Ireland Leinster Football Championship

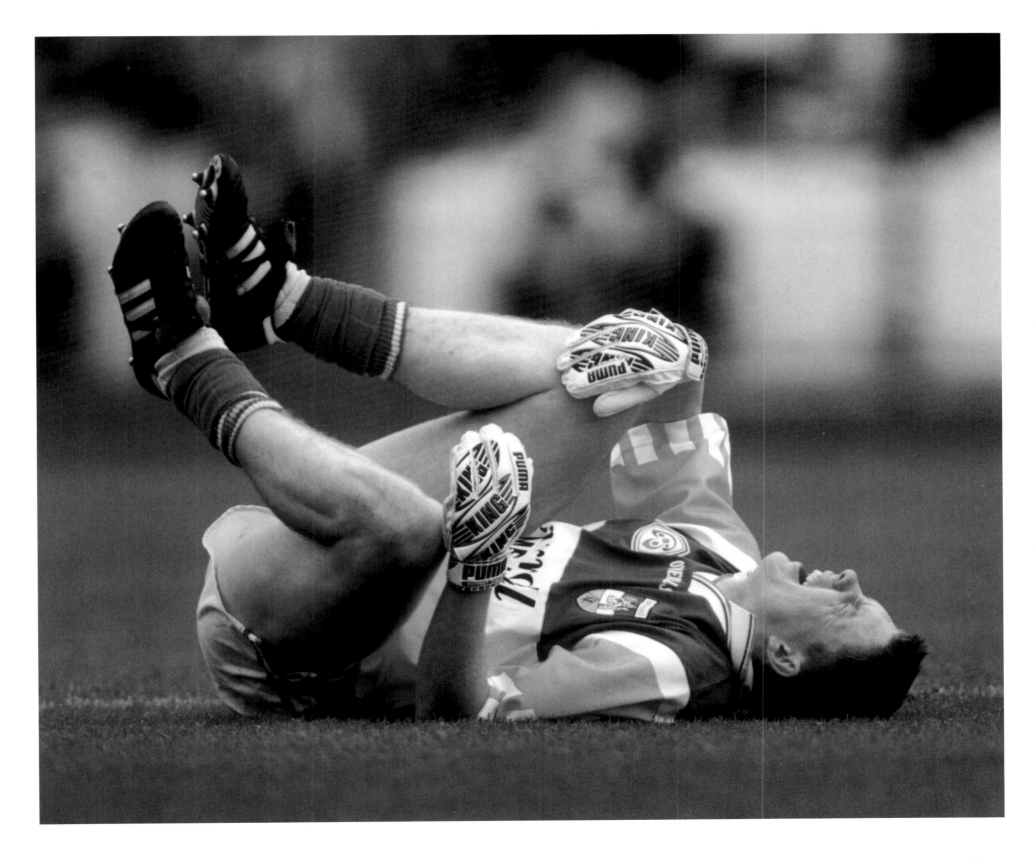

Bank of Ireland Ulster Football Championship   **Donegal 1-11 Antrim 0-11**

THE RAIN POURS DOWN AND DONEGAL DRIVE ON. JIM MCGUINNESS GETS A DISCERNING FIST TO THE BALL AHEAD OF CIARAN O'NEILL OF ANTRIM.

THE DEBATE OVER THE PRECISE NATURE OF THE TACKLE IN GAELIC FOOTBALL CONTINUES AS JASON CROTTY OF WATERFORD PUTS THE LOCK ON TIPPERARY'S MICHAEL SPILLANE.

SUMMER AND NOTHING BUT BLUE SKIES AND RICH BRASS. THE ARTANE BOYS BAND STRUT IT OUT ON THE NORTHSIDE.

Dublin 0-14 Kilkenny 4-23   Guinness Leinster Hurling Championship

CHARLIE CARTER OF KILKENNY BARS THE GATE ON SEÁN POWER OF DUBLIN WHILE NIALL MOLONEY WAITS IN ATTENDANCE.

*FOUR LEGS, FOUR ARMS, ONE HURLEY, NO BALL. SEÁN O'FARRELL OF CORK AND PA CAREY
OF LIMERICK LOCK LEGS, ARMS AND STARES, AS THEY TUSSLE FOR THE TIMBER.*

Derry 3-13 Monaghan 0-11   Bank of Ireland Ulster Football Championship

EARLY IN WHAT LOOKS LIKE BEING A BAD DAY AT THE OFFICE, EDWIN MURPHY
OF MONAGHAN IS SENT OFF BY REFEREE MICHAEL McGRATH.

May 31

Bank of Ireland Connacht Football Championship   **London 1-07 Sligo 0-14**

INTERNATIONAL RULES. BRITISH SPORTS MINISTER, TONY BANKS, M.P., IS INTRODUCED TO THE LONDON TEAM BY THEIR CAPTAIN BARRY McSHANE. A LONG LINE OF HANDSHAKERS FOLLOW.

SEÁN DAVEY OF SLIGO HOLDS OFF THE CHALLENGE OF LONDON'S TONY MURPHY AT RUISLIP.

Bank of Ireland Leinster Football Championship   **Laois 1-15 Westmeath 0-15**

MIDLANDERS BECOME AIRBORNE. TONY MAHER AND NOEL GARVAN OF LAOIS GO INTO ORBIT WITH DAMIEN GAVIN AND DAVID HUGHES OF WESTMEATH.

BRIAN STYNES OF DUBLIN IS STOPPED IN HIS TRACKS
BY KILDARE MIDFIELDER WILLIE McCREERY

June 7

Cumann na mBunscol Primary Game   **Tipperary 2-02 Waterford 0-01**

IT'S A BALL ALRIGHT. YOUNGSTERS SURVEY THE SLIOTAR DURING THE PRIMARY SCHOOLS GAME AT HALF TIME OF THE TIPPERARY V WATERFORD MUNSTER CHAMPIONSHIP CLASH.

Cavan 0-13 Fermanagh 0-11   Bank of Ireland Ulster Football Championship

CREW-CUT CELEBRATION. CAVAN GOALKEEPER PAUL O'DOWD GREETS THE FINAL WHISTLE AT BREFFNI PARK.

Guinness Munster Hurling Championship   **Waterford 0-21 Tipperary 2-12**

ON THE GOOD DAYS SUCCESS JUST BRINGS PEACE. STEPHEN FRAMPTON LEANS ON HIS HURLEY WHILE BILLY
O'SULLIVAN FEELS THE COOL OF THE WALL ON HIS BACK AFTER WATERFORD'S DEFEAT OF TIPPERARY.

BILLY O'SULLIVAN OF WATERFORD DIPS HIS HEAD AND
STRAINS HIS SINEWS TRYING TO GET THE YARD OF SPACE HE
NEEDS. COLM BONNAR OF TIPPERARY KEEPS STRIDE.

June 14

Guinness Leinster Hurling Championship   **Kilkenny 3-11 Laois 1-14**

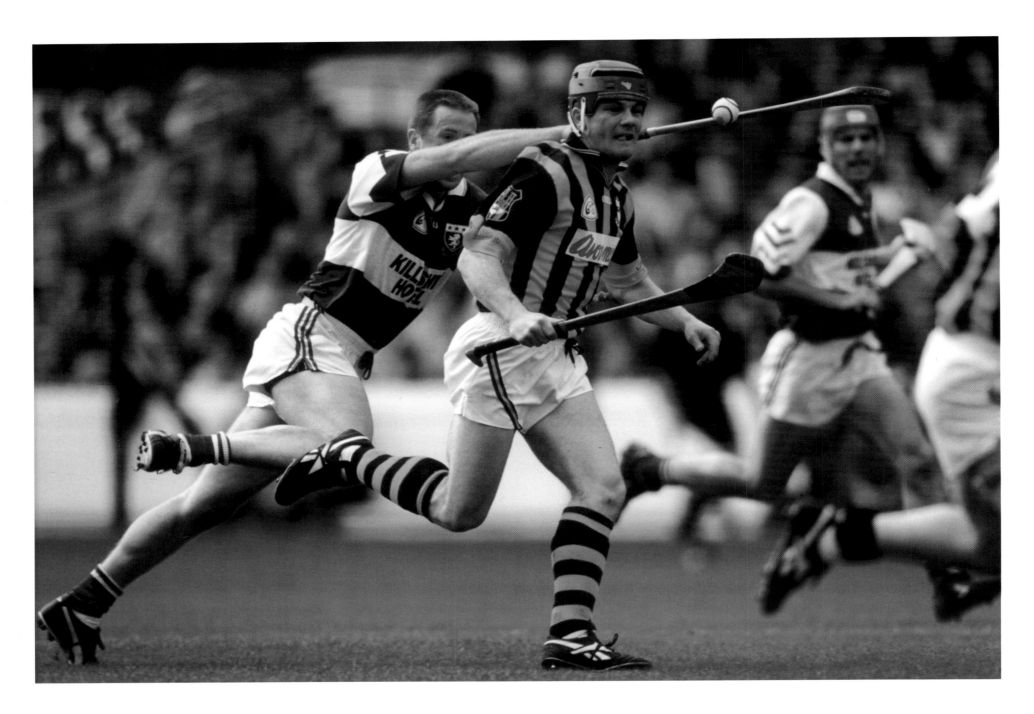

BUSINESS AS USUAL FOR NIALL MOLONEY OF KILKENNY AS HE CONTINUES OBLIVIOUS TO THE FRANTIC CHALLENGE OF NIALL RIGNEY OF LAOIS.

IN THE MOMENTS OF CALM BEFORE THE STORM. MICHAEL 'BABS' KEATING, THE OFFALY MANAGER, IMPARTS SOME WORDS OF ADVICE TO GARY HANNIFY.

THE ALLELUIA CHORUS BREAKS OUT AS JARLATH BURNS OF ARMAGH CELEBRATES HIS TEAM'S VICTORY OVER THEIR NEIGHBOURS DOWN.

ARMAGH'S JOINT-MANAGER, BRIAN MCALINDEN,
CELEBRATES DELIVERANCE FROM DOWN'S
DOMINANCE WITH HIS DAUGHTER MAIGHDLIN.

Bank of Ireland Leinster Football Championship   **Dublin 1-08 Kildare 0-12**

THE TEAM THAT PRAYS TOGETHER STAYS TOGETHER.   THE KILDARE PLAYERS AND OFFICIALS DO SOME

FUNDAMENTALIST WORSHIPPING AFTER THE FINAL WHISTLE AGAINST DUBLIN.

Dublin 1-08 Kildare 0-12   Bank of Ireland Leinster Football Championship

*ROBBIE BOYLE OF DUBLIN, WHOSE ONLY PREVIOUS
CHAMPIONSHIP APPEARANCE FOR HIS COUNTY HAD
EARNED HIM AN ALL-IRELAND MEDAL, ABSORBS HIS
NEW REALITY AS CHRISTY BYRNE AND SEAMUS
'SOS' DOWLING OF KILDARE CELEBRATE THEIRS.*

Bank of Ireland Ulster Football Championship   **Donegal 0-15 Cavan 0-13**

DERMOT MCCABE OF CAVAN, WITH THE GUMSHIELD IN THE COUNTY COLOURS, IS OUTNUMBERED BUT NOT OUTJUMPED BY JOHN GILDEA AND MANUS BOYLE OF DONEGAL. GERRY SHERIDAN AWAITS DEVELOPMENTS.

CLARE GOALKEEPER DAVY FITZGERALD STEPS OUT OF THE LINE TO DO WHAT HE DOES BEST. HE GETS THE TIMBER ONTO THE LEATHER WHILE FRANK LOHAN, LIAM DOYLE, BRIAN LOHAN AND SEÁN McMAHON LOOK ON APPRECIATIVELY.

SUMMER TIME AND THE LIVIN' IS EASY. AS CLARE CELEBRATE ANOTHER WIN, DAVY FITZGERALD AND LIAM DOYLE EMBRACE.

Meath 0-15 Louth 1-11   Bank of Ireland Leinster Football Championship

SUMMER IS AN ENDLESS SERIES OF SUNDAYS
WHERE THE WINNERS LEAVE THE LOSERS BEHIND.
DONAL CURTIS OF MEATH SAYS SO LONG AND
FAREWELL TO STEFAN WHITE OF LOUTH.

June 28

Bank of Ireland Connacht Football Championship   **Roscommon 2-12 Sligo 1-15**

SLIGO WING-BACK NIALL CLANCY CUTS THROUGH THE AIR AS FRANCIE GREHAN ARRIVES GASPING FOR IT IN THE CONNACHT CHAMPIONSHIP.

Derry 2-13 Armagh 0-12   Bank of Ireland Ulster Football Championship

HANDS HIGH, OLD STYLE. PAUL MCGRANE OF ARMAGH AND ENDA MULDOON OF DERRY FETCH FROM THE SKIES. ENDA MCNULTY STOPS SHORT BENEATH THEM.

June 28

Bank of Ireland Munster Football Championship   **Tipperary 1-16 Clare 0-12**

SENAN HEHIR, FORMERLY OF LONDON NOW OF CLARE, GETS TO SAMPLE THE TIPPERARY NO-LOOK TACKLE AS DEMONSTRATED BY NIALL KELLY.

Kerry 1-14 Cork 1-11   Bank of Ireland Munster Football Championship

DARA Ó SÉ OF KERRY HIGH STEPS IT TO SUCCESS AS DAMIEN O'NEILL, CORK, LOOKS TO MAKE THE KNOCKDOWN.

Guinness Leinster Hurling Final   **Kilkenny 3-10 Offaly 1-11**

BEFORE HE HAS EVEN BROKEN SWEAT, JOHN TROY OF OFFALY IS OPEN-ARMED AND CELEBRATING HIS GOAL IN THE SIXTH MINUTE.

KEVIN KINAHAN OF OFFALY CREASES HIS FACE IN CONCENTRATION AS HE STRAINS AHEAD OF CHARLIE CARTER AND ANDY COMERFORD IN THE RACE FOR THE SLIOTAR.

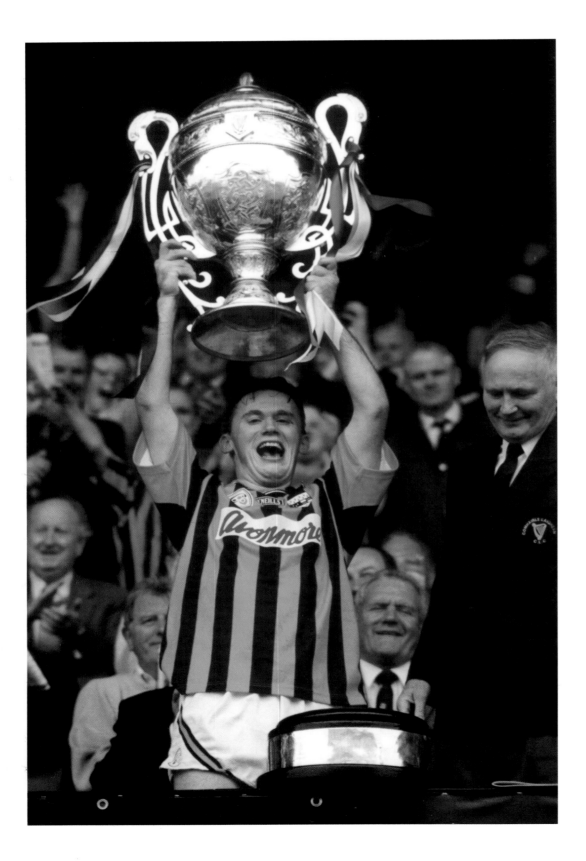

THROUGH THE FRONT DOOR. KILKENNY CAPTAIN TOM HICKEY LIFTS THE BOB O'KEEFFE CUP AS KILKENNY ADVANCE TO THE ALL-IRELAND SERIES AS LEINSTER CHAMPIONS.

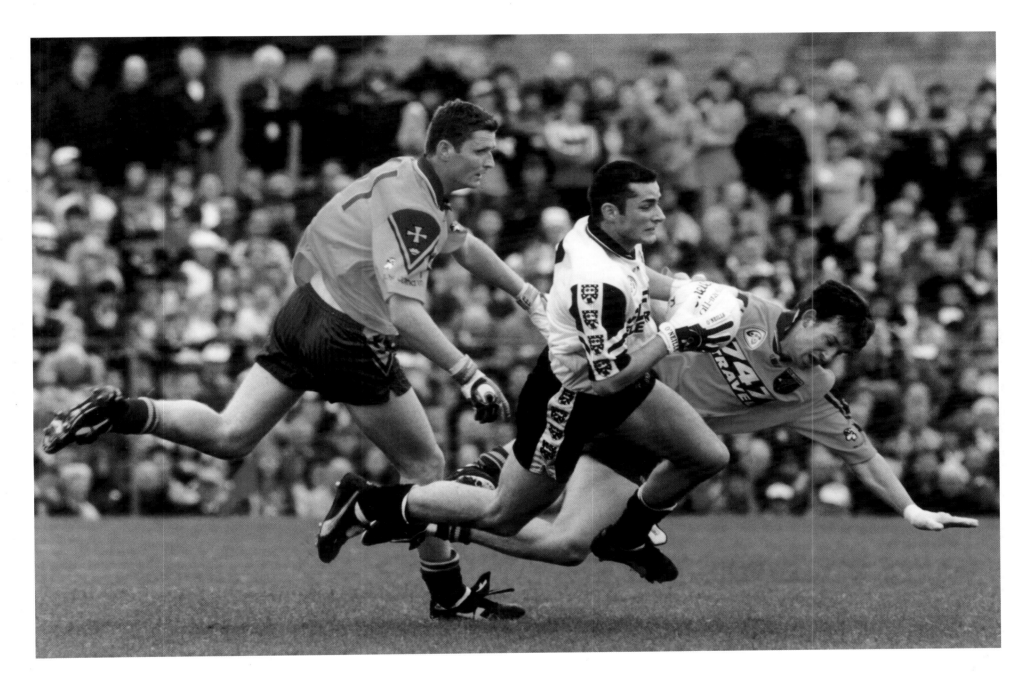

ONE FOOT ON THE GROUND. DON CONNELLAN OF ROSCOMMON IS THE ONLY ONE TO RETAIN CONTACT WITH

THE EARTH, AS SLIGO'S EAMONN O'HARA BURSTS PAST CLIFFORD McDONALD.

Clare 1-16 Waterford 3-10   Guinness Munster Hurling Final

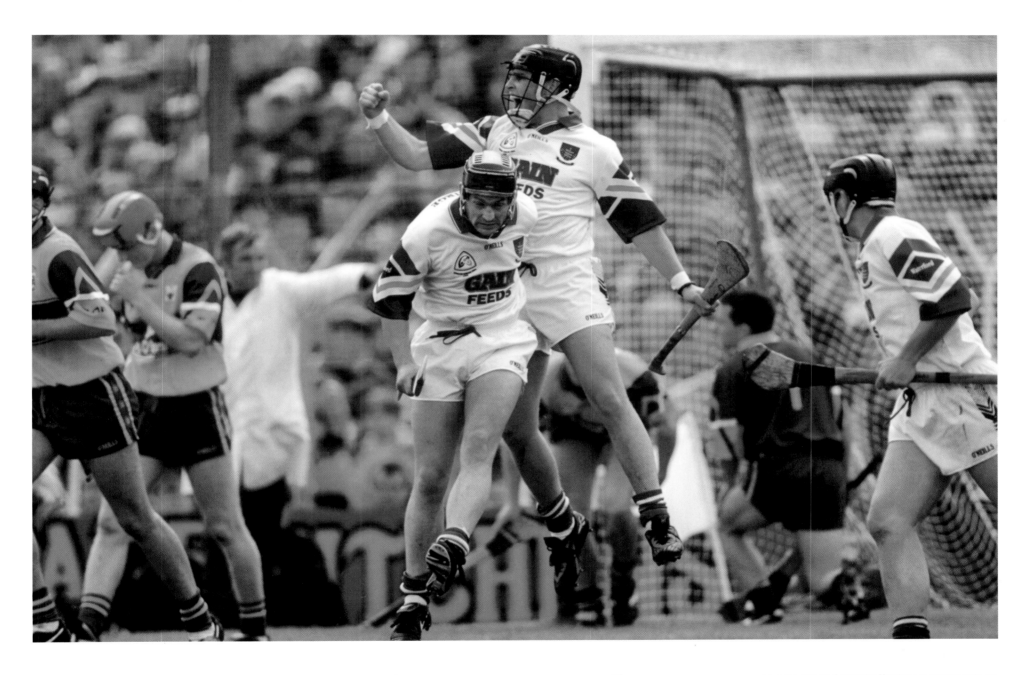

THE AFTERNOON BULGES WITH SUDDEN PROMISE AS ANTHONY KIRWAN LEAPS INTO THE AIR WITH FIST CLENCHED AFTER WATERFORD'S FIRST GOAL. TEAM-MATES BILLY O'SULLIVAN AND PAUL FLYNN KEEP THEIR FEET ON THE GROUND.

AS THE GAME GETS AWAY FROM THEM AGAIN, ROSCOMMON KEEP THE FAITH. MARK HEALY BENDS HIS HURLEY AROUND THAT OF KEVIN BRODERICK, WHO GETS HIS SHOT IN ANYWAY.

BRENDAN DEVENNEY HAS THE OFF-THE-SHOULDER LOOK FORCED ON HIM AS GARY COLEMAN OF DERRY WORKS HIS WAY TOWARDS THE BALL.

Derry 1-07 Donegal 0-08   Bank of Ireland Ulster Football Final

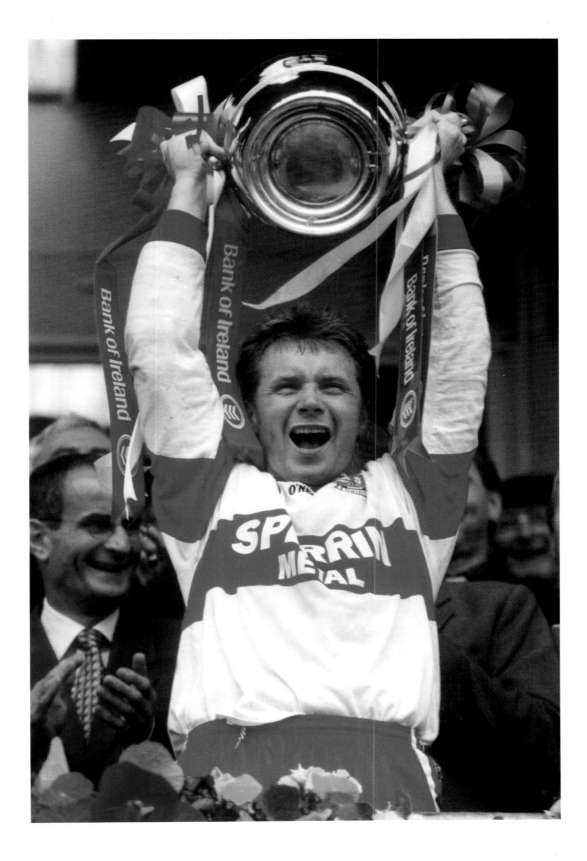

THE ULSTER CHAMPIONSHIP DRAWS TO A CLOSE AS KIERAN McKEEVER

LIFTS THE ANGLO CELT CUP ON BEHALF OF HIS TEAM.

July 19

Guinness Munster Hurling Final   **Clare 2-16 Waterford 0-10**

GLIDERS. ANTHONY KIRWAN OF WATERFORD BANKS TOWARDS THE LANDING AREA WITH THE BALL IN THE HOLD WHILE BRIAN QUINN DOES THE DOGFIGHTING.

Clare 2-16 Waterford 0-10   Guinness Munster Hurling Final

*CLARE FORWARD NIALL GILLIGAN CELEBRATES
THE GOAL WHICH SETS HIS TEAM ON THE WAY
TO ANOTHER MUNSTER CHAMPIONSHIP.*

OLD HAND MEETS NEW FACE. SEÁN McGUINNESS, MANAGER OF ANTRIM, OFFERS HIS BEST WISHES TO MICHAEL BOND AS HE TAKES CHARGE OF OFFALY FOR THE FIRST TIME.

GREEN UNSEEN. COLM CASSIDY OF OFFALY STICKS OUT A HAND AND A HURLEY AS ANTRIM'S KIERAN KELLY PULLS ON THE BALL.

Waterford 1-20 Galway 1-10 Guinness All-Ireland Hurling Quarter-Final

LOVE IS...AN ALL-IRELAND SEMI-FINAL APPEARANCE AFTER ALL THESE YEARS. PAUL FLYNN AND BRENDAN LANDERS CELEBRATE THEIR ARRIVAL IN THE BIG TIME.

SEÁN DALY OF WATERFORD AND LIAM HODGINS OF GALWAY MAKE TWIN TOWERS OF THEIR FOREARMS AS THEY TUSSLE FOR POSSESSION. DALY HAS THE EDGE.

Outnumbered by three to one, Galway's Padraic Joyce nevertheless gets a clear jump at the ball. Tom Ryan and Gerry Keane of Roscommon leap while Enon Gavin watches.

Galway 1-17 Roscommon 0-17   Bank of Ireland Connacht Football Final

TWO GAMES AND ONE HUNDRED AND SEVENTY MINUTES OF FOOTBALL LEAVE ROSCOMMON WITH NOTHING BUT MEMORIES. FERGAL O'DONNELL LAMENTS THE LOSS.

Bank of Ireland Leinster Football Final   **Kildare 1-12 Meath 0-10**

LILYWHITE TOP HAT AND SUMMER TALES. A YOUNG KILDARE FAN CELEBRATES THE RENAISSANCE.

MOMENTS LIKE THESE. THE KILDARE TEAM LINE UP BEHIND CAPTAIN GLEN RYAN AND THE ARTANE BOYS BAND BEFORE THE LEINSTER FINAL.

FOOTBALL IS A GAME OF GEOMETRY NIGEL NESTOR CONCENTRATES ON HIS ANGLES AS NIALL BUCKLEY JUDGES THE TRAJECTORY AND JOHN FINN CLOSES IN.

THE DEFINING MOMENT OF KILDARE'S SUMMER. AND MEATH'S. SUBSTITUTE BRIAN MURPHY BLASTS THE WINNING GOAL HOME UNDER THE BODIES OF DONAL CURTIS AND CONOR MARTIN.

Bank of Ireland Leinster Football Final   **Kildare 1-12 Meath 0-10**

HAPPY TIMES ARE HERE AGAIN AS KILDARE MANAGER MICK O'DWYER IS ENGULFED BY THE FAITHFUL, HAVING LED THEM FROM THE WILDERNESS.

Kildare 1-12 Meath 0-10   Bank of Ireland Leinster Football Final

A MOMENT TO TELL THE GRANDCHILDREN ABOUT. KILDARE CAPTAIN GLEN RYAN RAISES THE CUP WITH ANTHONY RAINBOW EXULTANT IN THE FOREGROUND.

*ALONE, ALL ALONE. AN OFFALY FAN IN THE
HOGAN STAND BEFORE THE GAME.*

Clare 1-13 Offaly 1-13   Guinness All-Ireland Hurling Semi-Final

ALONE IN THE CROWD. CLARE MANAGER GER LOUGHNANE
ISSUES INSTRUCTIONS TO HIS TEAM FROM THE FIRST ROW OF
THE NEW STAND IN CROKE PARK HAVING BEEN BANNED
FROM THE DUG-OUT. CLARE'S OTHER SUSPENSION
CASUALTY, BRIAN LOHAN, SITS BESIDE HIM.

 Guinness All-Ireland Hurling Semi-Final   **Clare 1-13 Offaly 1-13**

THROUGH GRITTED TEETH… FERGUS TUOHY OF CLARE
CELEBRATES HIS INFLUENTIAL GOAL AGAINST OFFALY.

WITH THE BALL DROPPING AS STEADILY AS THE SUN INTO THE HAND OF KEVIN KINAHAN, CLARE'S GER O'LOUGHLIN GETS SET TO TURN AND CHASE.

August 16

Guinness All-Ireland Hurling Semi-Final   **Kilkenny 1-11 Waterford 1-10**

THE BIG MAN BOWS TO THE BEATEN. PAT O'NEILL, KILKENNY'S BURLY FULL-BACK, BENDS TO
CONSOLE KEN McGRATH AFTER WATERFORD'S WONDERFUL SUMMER CAME TO AN END.

WITH THE BALL SKIMMING HALF AN INCH ABOVE THE TURF,
SEÁN DALY OF WATERFORD AND LIAM KEOGHAN OF
KILKENNY CHOP DOWN TO ARREST ITS PROGRESS.

Guinness All-Ireland Hurling Semi-Final   **Kilkenny 1-11 Waterford 1-10**

KILKENNY'S GOALSCORER NIALL MOLONEY
WELCOMES THE FINAL WHISTLE.

MEANWHILE...WATERFORD GOALIE BRENDAN LANDERS
GREETS THE FINAL WHISTLE WITH DESPAIR.

IN A MOVING CEREMONY OF COMMEMORATION, THE NAMES OF THE VICTIMS OF THE OMAGH BOMBING ARE READ OUT BY SCHOOLCHILDREN DRESSED IN DIFFERENT COUNTY COLOURS.

THE CLARE TEAM AND OFFICIALS JOIN THE CROKE PARK ATTENDANCE IN STANDING FOR A MINUTE'S SILENCE IN RESPECT FOR THE VICTIMS OF THE OMAGH BOMBING.

Guinness All-Ireland Hurling Semi-Final   **Clare 1-16 Offaly 2-10**

Clare 1-16 Offaly 2-10   Guinness All-Ireland Hurling Semi-Final

THE THIEF OF TIME STRIKES AS REFEREE JIMMY COONEY OUTSTRETCHES HIS ARMS AND BLOWS HIS WHISTLE TO INADVERTENTLY FINISH THE ALL-IRELAND SEMI-FINAL ALMOST THREE MINUTES EARLY.

DEAD SOLID PERFECT. JOHNNY DOOLEY OF OFFALY PREPARES TO MAKE

CONTACT AS NIALL GILLIGAN ARRIVES A SPLIT SECOND TOO LATE.

August 23

THE WORST OF TIMES. GALWAY'S GOALKEEPER MARTIN MCNAMARA FAILS TO STOP GARY COLEMAN OF DERRY FROM SCORING A GOAL FROM THE PENALTY SPOT.

Bank of Ireland All-Ireland Football Semi-Final **Galway 0-16 Derry 1-08**

Galway 0-16 Derry 1-08   Bank of Ireland All-Ireland Football Semi-Final

AND THE BEST OF TIMES. MARTIN MCNAMARA IS EMBRACED BY FRIEND AND CLUB-MATE JOE STEPHENS OF COROFIN AFTER THE FINAL WHISTLE USHERS GALWAY INTO THE ALL-IRELAND FINAL.

Guinness All-Ireland Hurling Semi-Final   **Offaly 0-16 Clare 0-13**

Offaly 0-16 Clare 0-13   Guinness All-Ireland Hurling Semi-Final

THE DAYS OF THEIR LIVES. AMID SUNSHINE AND SMILES, OFFALY MIDFIELDER, JOHNNY PILKINGTON, IS CARRIED SHOULDER HIGH FROM THE THURLES PITCH AFTER THE CLARE/OFFALY SAGA ENDS AT LAST.

CLARE CORNER-BACK BRIAN QUINN LEANS INTO THE
CHALLENGE OFFERED BY VETERAN JOE DOOLEY.

TURNING THE CHEEK #1. DAVY DALTON OF KILDARE BREAKS FOR THE BORDER WHILE MAURICE FITZGERALD CRACKS HIS CHEEK.

TURNING THE CHEEK #2. KILDARE GOALKEEPER CHRISTY BYRNE IS KISSED AND CONGRATULATED BY FANS.

Bord naGaeilge All-Ireland Camogie Final **Cork 2-13 Galway 0-15**

HELMETS, HURLEYS AND HEADBANDS AKIMBO AS FIONA O'DRISCOLL OF CORK REACHES FOR THE BALL AHEAD OF TRACY LAHEEN OF GALWAY.

Cork 2-13 Galway 0-15   Bord naGaeilge All-Ireland Camogie Final

*EITHNE DUGGAN, CAPTAIN OF CORK,
LIFTS THE ALL-IRELAND TROPHY.*

All-Ireland Minor Hurling Final   **Cork 2-15 Kilkenny 1-09**

Cork 2-15 Kilkenny 1-09   All-Ireland Minor Hurling Final

ANOTHER GENERATION OF CORK HURLERS
GRADUATE FROM THE MINOR RANKS AS
CAPTAIN CATHAL MCCARTHY RAISES
THE IRISH PRESS CUP.

JOHN COOGAN OF KILKENNY
CLOSES IN ON AN ATTEMPT TO
HOOK JAMES EGAN OF CORK
DURING THE MINOR FINAL.

Guinness All-Ireland Hurling Final **Offaly 2-16 Kilkenny 1-13**

THE PROTOCOL AND THE PRESSURE. THE PRE-GAME CEREMONY CONTINUES AS PRESIDENT MARY MCALEESE IS INTRODUCED TO OFFALY CAPTAIN HUBERT RIGNEY BY GAA PRESIDENT JOE MCDONAGH.

Offaly 2-16 Kilkenny 1-13   Guinness All-Ireland Hurling Final

ON YOUR MARKS.... DICKIE MURPHY OF WEXFORD THROWS THE SLIOTAR IN TO START THE ACTION IN THE ALL-IRELAND HURLING FINAL. PETER BARRY AND PHILIP LARKIN OF KILKENNY SWING AGAINST JOHNNY DOOLEY AND JOHNNY PILKINGTON OF OFFALY.

Guinness All-Ireland Hurling Final **Offaly 2-16 Kilkenny 1-13**

ALL EYES FOLLOW HIM. DJ CAREY CAPTURED AS A STUDY IN CONCENTRATION AS HE TAKES A FREE IN FRONT OF THE HOGAN STAND.

Offaly 2-16 Kilkenny 1-13   Guinness All-Ireland Hurling Final

WILLIE O'CONNOR OF KILKENNY, BEREFT OF HURLEY BUT NOT HOPE, CAN DO NOTHING TO STOP JOHNNY DOOLEY GALLOPING PAST, BALL IN HAND.

September 13

Guinness All-Ireland Hurling Final **Offaly 2-16 Kilkenny 1-13**

BRIAN WHELAHAN CROWNS HIS EXTRAORDINARY SEASON BY SCORING A LATE GOAL IN THE ALL-IRELAND FINAL. HE IS CONGRATULATED BY CLUB AND COUNTY TEAM-MATE JOE ERRITY. CANICE BRENNAN AND PAT O'NEILL OF KILKENNY WALK BACK TO PICK UP THE PIECES.

OFFALY'S DARREN HANNIFY COMES INTO THE LIGHT, CARRIED ON THE SHOULDERS OF SUPPORTERS AFTER THE ALL-IRELAND FINAL.

THE DREAMSTUFF. TWO YOUNG OFFALY SUPPORTERS WATCH FROM THE STAND AS THE LIAM McCARTHY CUP IS PRESENTED.

Offaly 2-16 Kilkenny 1-13   Guinness All-Ireland Hurling Final

THE END OF A TUMULTUOUS HURLING SEASON IS MARKED BY OFFALY CAPTAIN HUBERT RIGNEY RAISING THE LIAM McCARTHY CUP TO THE HEAVENS AND HURLERS AROUND THE COUNTRY VOWING TO DO THE SAME THING NEXT SEPTEMBER.

All-Ireland Minor Football Final   **Tyrone 2-11 Laois 0-11**

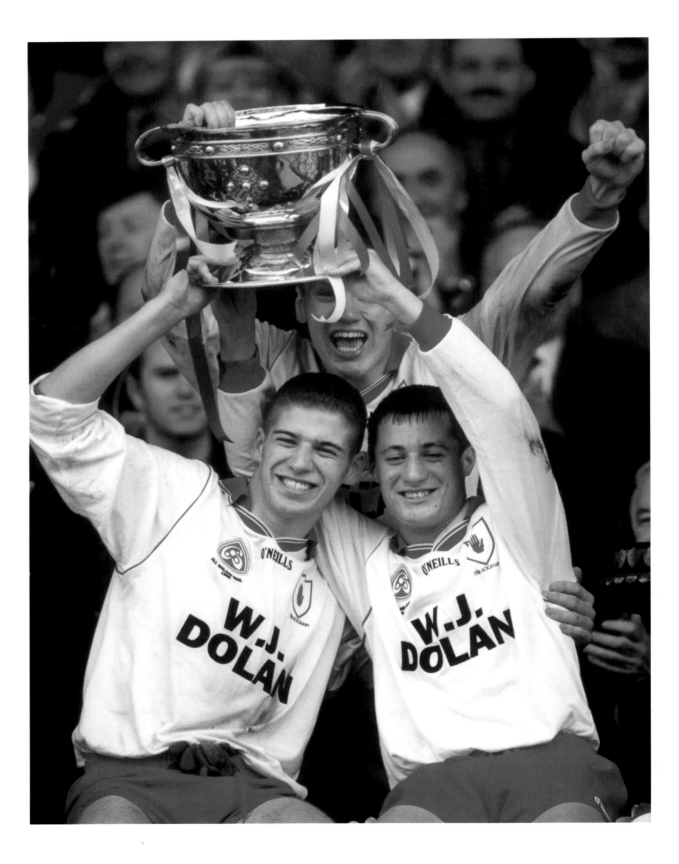

VICTORY CELEBRATION. CORMAC McANALLEN, TYRONE'S CAPTAIN FOR THE DAY, GETS A HAND RAISING THE TROPHY FROM KEVIN HUGHES AND BRIAN McGUIGAN. McGUIGAN HAD BEEN TEAM CAPTAIN FOR THE SEASON BUT INJURY KEPT HIM OUT OF THE STARTING FIFTEEN.

Tyrone 2-11 Laois 0-11   All-Ireland Minor Football Final

LAOIS PHENOMENON BRIAN MCDONALD MOURNS A LOST PIECE OF HISTORY. VICTORY IN THE FINAL WOULD HAVE GIVEN HIM THREE ALL-IRELAND MINOR MEDALS.

September 27

All-Ireland Minor Football Final   **Tyrone 2-11 Laois 0-11**

IN A WARM SPORTING GESTURE, WHICH RECOGNISES BOTH THE EFFORT OF THE CONQUERORS AND THE MEMORIES OF OMAGH, THE LAOIS MINOR TEAM APPLAUD TYRONE FROM THE FIELD IN CROKE PARK.

Galway 1-14 Kildare 1-10   Bank of Ireland All-Ireland Football Final

DOUBLE EUROPEAN GOLD MEDALLIST AND DOUBLE WORLD CROSS-COUNTRY CHAMPION, SONIA O'SULLIVAN, COMMENCES A LAP OF CROKE PARK BETWEEN THE MINOR AND SENIOR GAMES. THE RUN WAS TO HIGHLIGHT THE WORK OF THE THIRD WORLD RELIEF AGENCY GOAL.

September 27

LIFT OFF. REFEREE JOHN BANNON THROWS IN THE BALL TO START THE ALL-IRELAND FINAL. NIALL BUCKLEY OF KILDARE RISES WITH SEÁN O'DOMHNAILL AND KEVIN WALSH OF GALWAY.

Galway 1-14 Kildare 1-10   Bank of Ireland All-Ireland Football Final

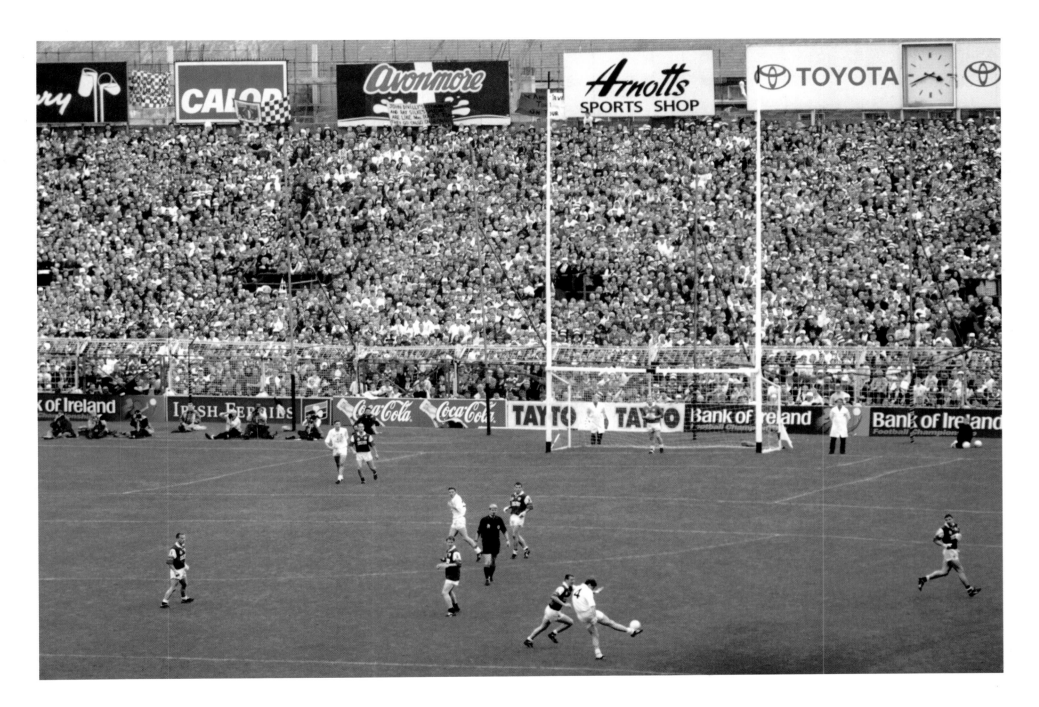

NOW YOU SEE IT. KARL O'DWYER, ONCE OF KERRY NOW OF KILDARE, KICKS FOR A POINT INTO THE CANAL END. DESTRUCTION OF THE TERRACE BEGAN THE WEEK AFTER THE FINAL.

September 27

Bank of Ireland All-Ireland Football Final   **Galway 1-14 Kildare 1-10**

FULL FRONTAL ASSAULT. TOMÁS MANNION OF GALWAY AWAITS POSSESSION AS SEÁN O DOMHNAILL AND DERMOT EARLEY COLLIDE IN MID-AIR.

TWO CAREERS INTERSECT. MICHAEL DONNELLAN, HAVING A GOOD DAY, BOUNDS AWAY FROM KILDARE'S BRIAN LACEY, WHO IS HAVING A NOT SO GOOD DAY.

Bank of Ireland All-Ireland Football Final **Galway 1-14 Kildare 1-10**

WITH HIS CUSTOMARY RESTRAINT AND CONTROL, GALWAY MANAGER, JOHN O'MAHONY, ACKNOWLEDGES THE FINAL WHISTLE, WHICH HAS BROUGHT TO AN END HIS OWN PERSONAL JOURNEY AS A MANAGER SEARCHING THE BIGGEST PRIZE.

Galway 1-14 Kildare 1-10   Bank of Ireland All-Ireland Football Final

THERE IS A SLIGHT SENSE OF DÉJÀ VU IN THE HOGAN STAND
AS RAY SILKE OF COROFIN AND GALWAY CLIMBS THE STEPS
TO RAISE ANOTHER ALL-IRELAND TROPHY ABOVE HIS HEAD.

Bank of Ireland All-Ireland Ladies Junior Football Final   **Louth 4-08 Roscommon 2-09**

Monaghan 4-07 Waterford 1-16   Bank of Ireland All-Ireland Ladies Senior Football Final

*NOIRÍN WALSH OF WATERFORD RISES ABOVE DIANE DEMPSEY
OF MONAGHAN BUT CAN'T GET A GLOVE TO THE BALL.*

*THE TROUBLES OF THE WORLD. DEJECTED ROSCOMMON
PLAYER DIANE DOLAN ALLOWS HERSELF A FEW TEARS
AFTER HER SIDE'S DEFEAT BY LOUTH.*

Coca-Cola International Series   **Ireland 4-12-07   Australia 2-10-14**

Having watched and learned, Wayne Carey of Australia takes a clean fetch ahead of Ireland's John Kenny.

HOME GAME AND A HOME WIN. IRISH CAPTAIN, JOHN MCDERMOTT, LIFTS THE INTERNATIONAL RULES TROPHY AFTER IRELAND DEFEAT AUSTRALIA ON AGGREGATE TO WIN THE SERIES, BECOMING THE FIRST TEAM TO ACHIEVE THAT FEAT WHILE PLAYING AT HOME.

Bank of Ireland All-Ireland Ladies Senior Football Final   **Waterford 2-14 Monaghan 3-08**

WE'VE GOT THE POWER... WATERFORD CORNER-FORWARD ÁINE WALL CELEBRATES THE END OF THE ALL-IRELAND LADIES FOOTBALL FINAL.

Waterford 2-14 Monaghan 3-08   Bank of Ireland All-Ireland Ladies Senior Football Final   *October 25*

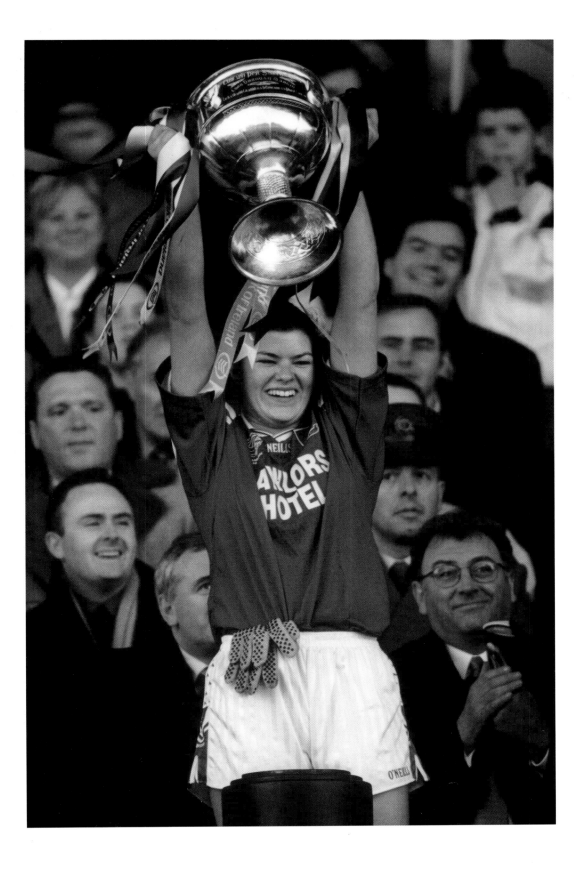

FINAL CHEER. THE LAST CROKE PARK CELEBRATION OF 1998 FINISHES AS SIOBHÁN O'RYAN, THE WATERFORD CAPTAIN, LIFTS THE BRENDAN MARTIN CUP. ALL-IRELAND LADIES CHAMPIONS AGAIN.